The Gentle Weapon

Prayers For Everyday And Not-So-Everyday Moments: Timeless Wisdom From The Teachings Of The Hasidic Master, Rebbe Nachman Of Breslov Adapted by Moshe Mykoff & S.C. Mizrahi with the Breslov Research Institute

EasyRead Large

Copyright Page from the Original Book

The Gentle Weapon: Prayers for Everyday and Not-So-Everyday Moments—
Timeless Wisdom from the Teachings of the Hasidic Master,
Rebbe Nachman of Breslov

2012 Quality Paperback Edition, Eighth Printing

Library of Congress Cataloging-in-Publication Data
Mykoff, Moshe.
The gentle weapon : prayers for everyday and not-so-everyday moments : timeless wisdom from the teachings of the Hasidic master, Rebbe Nachman of Breslov / adapted by Moshe Mykoff and S. C. Mizrahi together with the Breslov Research Institute.
p. cm.
Adaptation in English of selections from Likutey Moharan.
Includes index.
ISBN-13: 978-1-58023-022-3 (quality pbk.)
ISBN-10: 1-58023-022-9 (quality pbk.)
1. Hasidism. 2. Judaism—Prayer-books and devotions—English.
I. Nahman, of Bratslav, 1772–1810. Likutey Moharan. II. Mizrahi, S. C.
III. Breslov Research Institute. IV. Title.
BM198.2.M95   1998
296.4'5-dc21   98-47798
CIP

10 9 8

© 1999 by the Breslov Research Institute

Manufactured in the United States of America

Cover design: Bridgett Taylor
Cover illustration: Avi Katz
Text design: Glenn Suokko
Typesetting: Suzanne Church

For People of All Faiths, All Backgrounds
Published by Jewish Lights Publishing
A Division of LongHill Partners, Inc.
Sunset Farm Offices, Route 4, P.O. Box 237
Woodstock, VT 05091
Tel: (802) 457-4000   Fax: (802) 457-4004
www.jewishlights.com

TABLE OF CONTENTS

PROLOGUE

Rebbe Nachman said: "When you pray, hold nothing back from God. Pour out your heart with honest openness, as if you were speaking to your very best friend."

(Likutey Moharan 2:95)

Eternal Companion,
help us
pour out our hearts
to You
honestly and sincerely,
with these prayers
as our guide.
Help us
feel close
to You,
dear God.

DEDICATION

In memory of my father, Rabbi Isaac Nadoff—inspiration of my life; life of my inspiration; lifeline for so many.

SCM

In memory of Reb Shlomo—reaching the heart became much more difficult when you left this world.

MM

ACKNOWLEDGMENTS

To S.C., many thanks. Not only couldn't I have done this work without you, I *wouldn't* have done it without you.

My eternal gratitude to you, Elky—the award-winning co-author of my life.

MM

Thanks so much, MM. Your patient guidance has been my anchor.

My lifelong appreciation, MDM—for everything, forever. I could never have made it alone.

SCM

To Chaim Kramer, we are endlessly grateful for the wisdom and encouragement you so generously share.

NOTE ON SOURCES

Rebbe Nachman strongly urged his disciples to formulate their own prayers. He told them to build those prayers both on the topics they study in the holy books and on the everyday issues and experiences of their lives. In keeping with Rebbe Nachman's directive, the prayers in this collection deal with the familiar issues we all face, and are based on related teachings from the Rebbe's two-volume magnum opus, *Likutey Moharan* ("Collected Teachings of Rebbe Nachman"). Each prayer is thus followed by a source reference to the corresponding teaching found in that work. Some of the prayers found herein consist of two parts. These appear on facing pages, and the source follows the second part of the prayer, on the right-hand page.

INTRODUCTION

Life makes warriors of us all. To emerge the victors, we must arm ourselves with the most potent of weapons. That weapon is prayer.

—*Rebbe Nachman*

***

REBBE NACHMAN OF BRESLOV (1772–1810), spiritual master whose profound words and teachings have inspired generations of scholars and simple folk alike, always placed prayer at the core of all that he taught. "Give me your hearts," he said, "and I will take you on a new path that is in fact the old path on which our ancestors always walked—the path of prayer."

For thousands of years, people have prayed organized prayers, at established times, and in formal settings. Such prayers bolster us with the strength that comes from being linked to our traditions and roots.

Yet more than a link to the past, prayer brings us in touch with the here and now—with our innermost selves, and with the truth about all that we are and all that we are not.

And prayer brings us in touch with the future—with the possibilities of all we can become when we translate our hearts' most intimate longings into reality; when at last we achieve the wholeness that is the birthright of all humankind.

The secret of sincere prayer, Rebbe Nachman tells us, is to find those quiet moments when you can speak to God in the language of your heart—in your own words, in your own language. Established prayers were never intended to preclude the heartfelt cries that can well up at any time, in any place, in an outpouring of emotions from the depths of the soul.

By setting aside some time each day for focused, private prayer—which the Rebbe termed *hitbodedut*—we enter a special dimension of aloneness, in which the heart is open to intimate communion with God. "The new path that is in fact the old path" is then the most perfect path of the heart.

Ancient Jewish wisdom teaches that ultimately all of creation will reach a state of wholeness and perfection; the Messiah will unite the world with love, wisdom, and law. Said Rebbe Nachman: The Messiah will succeed in conquering the entire world without firing a shot. His will be the "gentle weapon" of prayer.

***

The prayers in this book are very personal responses, in the language of today, to experiences and issues we all face in today's world. The book's five sections encompass the basic elements of all human activity. These, the Kabbalists (Jewish mystics) tell us, are action, speech, feeling, thought, and will. Each corresponds to a level of the human soul, which in turn corresponds to a level of Creation. By focusing on these elements in our prayers, we can bind our inner soul with the transcendent Soul of Creation—and in this way draw nearer to God.

Each section begins with a prayer of praise to God and ends with a prayer of thanks. No relationship is a "one-way street." We cannot feel truly at one with our Creator if the sum total of our communication consists of requests for the things we want and need. Through prayers of praise and thanks, we "give" something back to God: we express our love for, and our dependence upon, the One Who is able to fulfill all our needs.

***

Use this book to help you summon the wherewithal to face the constant, ongoing battles of life. Read it for a moment here, an hour there. Cultivate your strongest, deepest emotions, and turn with them to God. Offer God all that your heart holds, and reap immeasurable returns. Turn to this book again and again to help you form the words your heart yearns to say.

And when you find your own words to express the outpourings of your heart, close this book and let those words flow. When you approach God in this way, your life will change dramatically for the better.

Although no one is spared life's struggles, we can face them without fear, armed with prayer.

Rebbe Nachman's foremost disciple, Reb Noson, prayed, "Master of the Universe! Help me make the words of my mouth one with my heart.... Help me express all I need to say before You in wholehearted truth!" Let us learn to confront life's battles wielding the gentle weapon of prayer, infused with all the truth and feeling our hearts and our souls possess.

1

ACTIONS

ACTIONS

NO PLACE TOO FAR

"First tell me this: Is there some secluded spot in the vicinity where I can go to pray?" Rebbe Nachman asked. He had just arrived in Breslov, the town whose name the Breslov movement has borne ever since.

"I know of a place that would be most suitable," the Hasid replied, "but it's quite far from here."

"Far?" the Rebbe exclaimed. "What do you mean by 'far'? Far from the mind ... or from the heart?"

Rebbe Nachman later taught: When your heart yearns, distance is no obstacle.

***

2

IN PRAISE

My God,
I work and I strive,
never knowing
if I will succeed.
You and only You
can give hope to my dreams.
With Your help
I am spared
wasted efforts.
With Your blessing,
all the hardship I endure
can bear fruit.
You and only You
are the key to success
in all that I do.

(LM 1:56)

COURAGE TO GROW

Almighty God,
Source of
all the energy of life,
without You I am helpless.
Give me the courage—
the physical drive,
the emotional energy,
and the spiritual will—
to risk in order to grow,
to welcome every challenge
as my life unfolds.

(LM 1:152)

A FULL LIFE

O Life of the World,
grant me a full life—
a life which may be considered long
because it has been filled with
right living,
and considered rich
because it has been filled with
holy acts.

(LM 1:60)

MAKING ENDS MEET

Source of all sustenance,
sustain me.
Nowadays,
even living simply—
working only
to acquire life's
most basic necessities,
demands so much.

IN THE BLACK

Help me see my way out of
this monstrous tangle of debts:
the inevitable outlay
for my children's needs;
those overwhelming expenses and bills;
those inescapable medical expenditures;
But most of all,
dear God,
help me keep my account with You
in the black!

(LM 1:172)

BODY & SOUL

Holy One,
grant me the strength
to cast off
the spiritual sluggishness
and indifference
which encumber my body.
Let my body—
together with my soul—
soar
ever closer
to You.

(LM 1:22)

TEACHING BY BEING

Dear God,
teach me to embody those ideals
I would want my children
to learn from me.
Let me communicate
with my children wisely—
in ways
that will draw their hearts
to kindness, to decency
and to true wisdom.
Dear God,
let me pass on to my children
only the good;
let them find in me
the values
and the behavior
I hope to see in them.

(LM 2:7)

WHOLENESS AND WELL-BEING

God of wholeness,
God of healing,
envelop us
with wholeness
and well-being.
Heal us in body and soul.
Let all the elements of our bodies
work together
in perfect symmetry
and in peaceful harmony.
Remove every trace of illness,
every hint of infirmity;
send the healing
which You alone can bring.

(LM 2:1)

SINCERITY

O You Who are infinitely Deep
yet also
profoundly Simple,
help me walk the simple path.
Free me
of any facade of sophistication,
which will only hinder
my endless quest
to come closer to You.
Help me live my life
with faith,
with sincerity
and with perfect simplicity.

(LM 2:19)

GIVING

My God, help me become a "giver."
Help me give ... and go on giving.
You've called on us
to be charitable;
show me how.
Show me how to give
with a pure heart,
with an open heart,
with a heart filled with joy.
Lead me to those
who are truly deserving,
for giving is so holy an act.
Help me find the truly needy,
and help them find me.

(LM 1:251)

TRUE NOURISHMENT

Dear God,
teach me to eat right,
and to eat for the right reasons.
Keep me
from eating the wrong foods,
and from eating more than I should.
Let all that I eat
nourish me,
never weaken
or harm me.
Let the food I ingest
create a perfect balance within me
in body,
mind
and soul.

(LM 1:263)

GAINING PERSPECTIVE

Dear God,
I need Your guidance.
Bring perspective to my life,
for the meaningless allures
of this world
control me.
Let me see beyond
the coarse requirements
of my daily subsistence.
Let me bask
in that which is truly precious—
in the beauty of my relationship
with You, dear God.

WORKING TO LIVE

Though I have no choice
but to work
to support myself
and those who depend on me,
let my job never dominate
my life
and psyche.
Let me never be so caught up
in the pursuit of my livelihood
that I stoop
to dishonesty
in order to get ahead.
Let me make no transaction
without recognizing
that any measure of success
I might find
can come only from You.

(LM 1:13)

STRESS

O God,
see my pain.
See the constant tension
and anxiety
with which I must function—
with which I *don't* function.
Touch my life
with Your love,
with Your strength,
with Your wisdom.
I have more than I can bear
alone.

(LM 1:54)

TROUBLES

Kind, loving, mighty God:
Stretch out Your hand
to strengthen me.
Lift me up
from my abyss;
right my wrongs;
turn my every failure
into success.
Look upon all my troubles
and say,
"Enough!"

(LM 1:195)

PRIORITIES

O God,
help me fix within my mind
the enduring truths of life.
Let my every action be directed
toward life's ultimate goals.
For how can I face You,
my Creator,
without having invested all my days
in preparation for that Moment
when I will meet You?
How can I face You,
Source of my life,
so long as I remain
naked and barren,
mired in the fantasies
that form the substance
of life's illusions?

(LM 1:54)

LIVING TO THE FULLEST

Dear God,
as I age—
as hours turn to days,
days to weeks,
weeks to months,
and months to years—
let none of my time
be wasted or lost.
Let me use my life
to the fullest,
to become the person
I am meant to be.

(LM 1:60)

IN THANKS

Dear God,
all the good
I can do in this world
will never match
all the good
You've done for me.
All my acts of kindness
will never equal
all the kindness
You've shown me.
Even all the gratitude I can muster
will never suffice
to express
my appreciation
and thanks
to You, my God.

(LM 2:78)

2

WORDS

Words

REBBE NACHMAN'S "MANTRA"

"I want to pray, to tell God everything I'm going through, and ask for help," a Hasid explained to Rebbe Nachman, "but when I'm finally alone and try to pray, the words don't come."

"Then," the Rebbe assured him, "even just calling out to God, *'Ribbono shel Olam!*[1]—again and again—is extremely beneficial."

Once, when informed that someone was able to recite a thousand pages of Talmud, Reb Noson responded, "Yes, that is impressive. Yet there are those of the Rebbe's followers who can repeat the phrase *'Ribbono shel Olam'* a thousand times!"

***

---

[1] [Hebrew, literally: "Master of the Universe"]

IN PRAISE

Master of the Universe!
You listen to the anguished cries
and desperate wails
of every one of
Your beloved children.
You hear my incoherent cries,
You comprehend my jumbled words.
I try my best to reach You;
with my inadequate prayers
I call out to You,
and You understand.

(LM 2:46)

PRAYER

God of life,
help me pray
with all the force I can muster.
If only I could invest all my energy
into each word
—even into every letter—
of my prayers,
I know that it would give me
renewed strength...
renewed spirit.
"Prayer to the Almighty is my life,"
says the Psalmist.
Please,
help me pray.

(LM 1:9)

CRYING OUT TO GOD

Oh, how I want to cry out to You,
God of strength,
to cry undistracted
and with a pure heart.
Help me pray
with all my strength,
to raise my voice
in resounding supplication—
until
my own prayers
strike my mind like thunderclaps,
and refine the innermost recesses
of my heart.

(LM 1:5)

ONE TRUE WORD

O dear God,
for once
let me call out to You with
one true prayer.
Let me
think
one pure thought,
cry
one genuine cry,
pray
one absolutely sincere prayer
to You
dear God.

(LM 1:30)

PRAYER FOR HEALING

God of wholeness,
God of healing,
hear our words,
accept our prayers;
send a special blessing
of healing
to (**name**) son/daughter of
(**mother's name**),
among all those of Your children
who are in need
of Your healing blessing.

(LM 2:1)

OPENNESS

Dear God,
I want
to open myself to You—
wholly,
perfectly
and sincerely.
I want
to tell You
about
my doubts—my certainties,
my weaknesses—my strengths,
my failures—my successes.

BREAKING DOWN THE BARRIERS

God,
I want to break down
every barrier
that separates me
from You.
I want to lay out before You
the parts of myself I love,
and the parts I despise;
the parts of myself that are healthy,
and the parts that need healing;
the parts I feel secure enough to speak of,
and the insecurities
I haven't the courage to share.

(LM 2:25)

CRYING AND SIGHING

The years have brought
more pain
than ever I imagined possible.
When I cry,
loving God,
let me cry only to You.
When I sigh,
let that sigh
be a pure, honest expression
of a soul yearning
for Your Light.

CRYING AND SIGHING

Let my cries and sighs
heal me
and restore me
and bring me to joy.
Let me never again succumb
to bitterness
or depressing thoughts.
God,
show me life's meaning.

(LM 1:56)

EFFECTIVE WORDS

God of wisdom,
teach me the right words.
Teach me the very words
that will touch the hearts
and souls
of others.
When a friend needs
my understanding ear,
teach me the words to say
that will strengthen,
that will encourage,
that will express
only my love
and concern.

(LM 1:34)

EFFECTIVE SILENCE

God of wisdom,
teach me to relate to others
with words they need to hear,
with words
that will never
misguide.
Teach me, dear God,
that often
the most effective words
are no words at all.
Teach me how and when
to communicate
with that most potent gift
of silence.

(LM 2:7)

SENSITIVE SPEECH

God of understanding,
guide me,
for my own words sometimes
baffle me.
When I relate to those around me
insensitively;
when I hurt,
embarrass
or insult them;
when I speak with a callousness
that causes pain;
when I lose myself
in my own ego—
God, pull me back to reality.
Help others understand
that I too am in pain,
and let them be forgiving.

(LM 2:1)

HARMFUL WORDS

O God,
help me avoid
every abuse of speech.
Let no untrue word
escape my lips.
I pray that I never
speak badly of others,
or speak empty words of flattery.
Help me stay away from profanity.
Teach me, dear God,
when to keep silent
and when to speak;
and when I speak O God,
save me from using
Your wonderful gift of speech
to humiliate or hurt
anyone.

(LM 1:63)

LIES

Ruler of the World,
grant me truth!
Spare me from the lies of others.
Help me stop myself
from lying
to others.
Save me
from lying to myself,
and spare me
from the lies
of my own illusions.
O God,
never let me live a lie,
even for only a moment.

(LM 1:7)

HOLY SOUNDS

O God,
Your creation resonates
with holy sounds.
Let me hear them all.
Let them penetrate my heart
and rouse my senses:
the jangle of a charity box;
the voice of a faithful teacher;
even the intonation
of my own sigh
when I cry out to You—
all these sounds are holy.
O God,
let my heart hear them all
and be uplifted.

(LM 1:22)

IN THANKS

God, ever my only Support,
You've taught me to pray—
to sigh,
to cry,
to awaken true, meaningful words
from deep within:
words that strengthen;
words that ease my pain
and heal my wounds;
words that dispel darkness.
Thank You, God,
for opening my lips
and for teaching me
to seek You
through prayer.

(LM 1:11)

3

FEELINGS

FEELINGS

PRAYING FOR WHAT YOU NEED

Rebbe Nachman taught: When it comes to praying for what you need, there is nothing too insignificant to ask of God.

Reb Noson once happened to mention to Rebbe Nachman some minor convenience that he was lacking."Then ask God to give it to you," the Rebbe advised him.

"I was completely astounded," Reb Noson relates."I would never have considered turning to God for something so trivial, which in any case I could have managed without.

"Noting my surprise, the Rebbe added, 'Tell me, is it beneath your dignity to pray for something so minor? No matter what you need, the best thing you can do is to pray for it.'"

***

IN PRAISE

Dear God of compassion,
Your mercies are with me always—
every moment of my life,
with each breath I take.
Only You can love me
so completely,
so unconditionally,
so profoundly.
If people care for me,
it is only because You care for me.
If any of my words
find their way
into the hearts of others,
it is nothing more than a reflection
of Your all-encompassing presence
in my life.

(LM 1:1)

COMPASSION

Loving God,
You Who are full of compassion,
teach me to be like You.
Teach me to be kind and generous
and loving,
just as You are kind and generous
and loving
to all Your creations.
Please
help me develop true sensitivity
and genuine compassion
toward everything in Creation.

(LM 1:105)

JOY

God,
I stand beaten and battered
by the countless manifestations
of my own inadequacies.
Yet we must
live with joy—
overcome despair,
seek, pursue and find
every inkling of goodness,
every positive point within ourselves,
and so discover true joy.
Aid me in this quest, O God.
Help me find satisfaction
and a deep, abiding pleasure
in all that I have,
in all that I do,
in all that I am.

(LM 1:282)

A POSITIVE ATTITUDE

Merciful God,
let me experience Your mercy.
Save me from pessimism,
from bitterness
and from cynicism.
Help me
overcome
my negative feelings;
help me
avoid
every form of arrogance,
every hint of greed.

LOVING PROTECTION

Loving God,
protect me with
Your love.
Prevent others
from viewing me with hostility.
Never allow
the negativity of others
to influence my life
or affect my destiny.

(LM 1:54)

SEEING THE GOOD

God, it is oh, so simple
to find the evil,
the ugly,
the bad.
Help me learn
to discount all that is negative
in the other.
Show me the goodness,
the beauty,
the kindness
in everyone I meet.

THE POWER OF LOVE

Teach me to search for the fine qualities
in others,
to recognize their immeasurable worth.
Teach me to cultivate a love
for all Your children,
for no one,
no one
is without
redeeming value.
Let the good in me
connect with the good
in others,
until all the world
is transformed through
the compelling power
of love.

(LM 2:17)

A SOUL MATE

O loving God,
so many in Your world
live without
true love,
so many
cannot find
their soul mate.
Have mercy on them.
O Source of all love,
let every lonely and incomplete soul
know the wholeness of being
that comes
when one finds
one's true love.

(LM 2:87)

LIVING IN LOVE

God of mercy, God of love,
it is sometimes difficult—
so painfully difficult—
to sustain a harmonious home life,
to maintain a marriage
based on
true friendship and love.
Let never a hint
of argument, frustration or suspicion
cloud our relationship.
We need
an extra measure of compassion
to understand
and to care for one another
with genuine sensitivity
and with open acceptance.
Let abundant peace fill our home.

(LM 2:87)

PEACE

God,
help me learn to cherish peace,
to pursue peace,
to promote peace.
Save me
from the need to be always
right—
which leads only to
tension
and strife.

ONENESS

God, help me
forge a oneness—
between myself and others;
between myself and my spouse;
between myself and my children.
Help me forge a oneness
of the many selves
within me.
Help me become one
with You.

(LM 1:75)

LEARNING TO WAIT

God of patience,
teach me
patience.
Help me learn
to wait—
for the good
that is just around the corner;
for the assistance
that will soon be within my reach;
for the relief
that is just a moment away.

INNER CALM

Patient God,
teach me to be patient—
unruffled by those who anger,
tolerant of those who exasperate,
accepting of those who disappoint.
Help me remain
serene in the face of derision,
calm in the face of provocation,
composed in the midst of a storm.
And, God...
teach me to be patient
with myself.

(LM 1:155)

FORGIVING

O forgiving God,
You alone know
how urgently I need to learn
to forgive.
Help me douse all the anger
that burns within me.
Free me of resentment
against those who have
wronged me.
Help me abandon
all the animosity,
all the hostility
that clogs my heart.
Help me turn my anger into love,
and my enmity into
compassion.

(LM 1:18)

ANGER

God,
I never want to become angry.
Protect me
from my own passions.
Don't let me lose myself to
small-mindedness
or resentment of others.
Guard me from turning my temper
against anything
or anyone—
even and especially
against
myself.

(LM 1:59)

A PEACEFUL DISPOSITION

Teach me, O God,
to seek only peace.
Save me from
every form of
argument, controversy and quarrel;
liberate me from
every type of
misunderstanding
and strife.
Where there is no peace,
there can be no joy,
there can be no love,
there can be no true
presence of mind.
Dear God,
let peace be mine to share.

(LM 1:80)

CONTENTMENT

Dear God,
save me from wanting
what is not mine.
Protect me from my own jealousy,
from desiring
the money or the possessions,
the position or the honor
that belong to another.
Let me trust in You
enough to believe
that what is meant to be mine
will come to me.
Let me trust in You
enough to be satisfied
with all that I have
today.

(LM 1:23)

SELF-ESTEEM

Dear God,
let me feel close to You.
Grant me satisfaction with my life.
Let me rejoice in that closeness,
and let me turn that satisfaction
into a sense of self-worth—
not one based in arrogance
or in feelings of self-importance,
but a humble self-esteem
rooted in holiness.

(LM 1:22)

ARROGANCE

Dear God,
free me of false pride;
free me of the arrogance
that accompanies an inflated self-image.
Spare me from haughtiness,
from the overloaded ego
which stems from an empty self.
Let me learn to feel good
about myself;
let me never feel the need
to belittle anyone
in order to find
value and worth,
in order to feel
valued and worthy.

(LM 1:14)

A HAVEN OF JOY

Teach me the meaning of joy,
dear God—
strong,
deep,
genuine
and pure joy.
Don't let me succumb
to feelings of sadness,
loneliness and depression.
Teach me to turn to You
with my every problem,
frustration,
anxiety and pain.
Accept my broken heart.
Heal me,
and shelter me
in a haven of joy.

(LM 1:24)

CLAPPING AND DANCING

Dear God,
stir my heart
with the spirit of joy.
Imbue my arms and my legs
with that spirit;
for my arms are encumbered
and my legs have become heavy
with my wrongdoings.
Fill me, my God,
with the cleansing spirit of holy joy.
Enliven all my limbs.
Help me raise my hands
and clap.
Help me lift my feet
and dance, dance, dance.

(LM 1:10)

OVERCOMING LOSS

Dear God,
suddenly I'm alone; I'm in pain.
As I search for some source
of comfort,
the world—
the world so full, so bustling—
seems so empty now.
It's cold
and it's frightening
in this hollow that is me—
in this hollow that once brimmed
with confidence and joy.
God, pull me back—
back to the world of the living,
back to a life of action
and human relationships.

(LM 1:277)

IN THANKS

Loving, caring God,
all the happiness and fulfillment
in my life
come only from You.
Knowing how absolute
is my dependence on You,
I find peace of mind.
Your presence
suffuses my life,
caressing me with
hope, joy and love.
I've tasted Your love,
I've known Your compassion,
I've experienced Your patience,
and I am filled with
gratefulness.

(LM 2:10)

4

THOUGHTS

THOUGHTS

AN ENTIRELY NEW WORLD

"It is impossible to describe how wonderful it was in those early years," Rebbe Nachman said to the Hasid. They were strolling through the outskirts of the village where the Rebbe had spent the first years of his marriage worshiping and serving God in relative anonymity. "With each step I took in these fields, praying and calling out to God, I experienced yet another taste of paradise."

On another occasion, Rebbe Nachman described what it was like returning home after a day spent crying his heart out to God in the fields or forest: "Coming back, everything appeared different to me. The world seemed entirely new."

***

IN PRAISE

O God,
I only begin to realize
how very much You've done for me.
I must now internalize
the understanding that
everything that happens to me
—everything—
is an expression of
Your everlasting love,
and Your concern
for my ultimate good.
God, as I recognize
all Your goodness,
as Your kindness
fills my thoughts,
I sing Your praise.

(LM 1:4)

LIGHT OF AWARENESS

God,
let me comprehend
all that I see
with the light of awareness.
Let me understand
whatever touches my life
in a deep and intimate way—
in a way
that embraces both
the adult
and the child
within me.

(LM 1:20)

ENVELOPED IN FAITH

My God,
You and only You know
how strongly I want
to believe in You,
to put all my faith
in You alone.
Help me make this desire
a reality.
Help me perceive
Your Presence
and draw strength from it
every moment of my life,
through every trial I face.
Let that recognition bolster
my faith in You—
wherever I go,
whatever I do.

(LM 2:44)

ACCEPTING GOD'S JUSTICE

God, help me see;
help me understand
all that I see
in the light of Your truth,
in the light of Your ultimate justice.
When I see the success of the wicked,
help me realize
that it is but an illusion—
nothing authentic,
nothing real.
Real success,
true good, absolute happiness,
are found only with You,
dear God of truth,
and one day I will see it,
experience it
and know it.

OVERCOMING DOUBTS

My vision is distorted,
loving God of truth.
I want to see clearly,
but my heart leads me
through twisted, convoluted paths
of misunderstood impressions.
Straighten those paths
so that I can strengthen myself
in the conviction of my beliefs.

(LM 1:55)

LEARNING LIFE'S LESSONS

Dear God,
let my heart
grasp
the profound wisdom
with which You created
the world.
Help me understand
that life's difficulties
are in fact her opportunities;
life's endings
are also her beginnings;
life's disappointments
are her finest teachers.

LEARNING LIFE'S LESSONS

Dear God,
let my heart
grasp
the profound wisdom
with which You created
me.
Help me understand
that my vulnerabilities
in fact open me to growth;
my limits
draw me to new frontiers;
my very failures
teach me to succeed.

(LM 1:18)

PERCEPTION: BODY AND SOUL

Holy One,
grant me the wisdom
to bring harmony
to the alliance
of my body and my soul.
Let them rise together
in my devotion to You.
My soul perceives Your light—
let my body discern it too.
My soul sounds Your praise—
let my body sing it too.

(LM 1:22)

FOCUSED PRAYER

O dear God,
how I want
to pray,
but the distractions
are never-ending.
Please—
help me overcome them.
Help me be
wholly focused.
For once
help me pray
only true,
totally heartfelt words
to You,
dear God.

(LM 1:30)

WISE COUNSEL

O God,
how can I make my way through
the confusion
and uncertainty
that cloud so much of what I do?
Guide me to wise teachers and mentors,
whose advice is pure
and in tune with Your Will.
Guide me to true friends,
whose counsel is caring
and promotes my best interests.
Guide me to clear, correct decisions,
to conclusions that are sound
and free of all doubt.

CLARITY AND ASSURANCE

O God,
grant me clarity
and assurance
in whatever I do.
Teach me to trust in wise teachers—
to learn from their insightful words.
Teach me to trust in true friends—
to treasure their care and concern.
Teach me to trust in myself—
to judge my own course
correctly,
and so to live
with conviction
and hope.

(LM 1:61)

MIRACLES OF NATURE

Dear God,
open my eyes
to see
the countless amazing miracles
You perform for me
constantly.
Open my mind
to understand
that what appears to be
the natural order of things
is in truth miraculous
in every way.
Your guiding Hand
directs and empowers me
in everything I do.

RECOGNIZING LIFE'S MIRACLES

Open my eyes,
O God,
to the marvels that surround me.
Show me the wonder
of each breath I take,
of my every
thought,
word
and movement.
Let me experience the miracles
of the world I witness—
ever mindful
and always appreciative
of all that You have made.

(LM 1:9)

SEEING LIGHT IN DARKNESS

God of unfathomable goodness,
the history of human agony
haunts my soul;
ashes, blood, and cries
pierce my heart;
diabolic schemes of oppressors
plague my mind.
Grant me an extra measure of
strength,
understanding
and faith
to help me find You—
to discover Your Light
midst the blinding dread,
through the revolting horror.

(LM 1:250)

SORTING THROUGH CONFUSION

God of truth,
help me sort through
the dizzying confusion
of my life.
My mind swirls with
all that I've seen,
all that I've read,
all that's happened to me.
Teach me to focus,
to prioritize,
to see with clarity,
so that I can move on
with my life.

(LM 1:15)

A HUMBLE SPIRIT

Dear God,
guide me along the path
of sincere humility.
If ever I put on airs—stop me!
Bless me with a humble spirit:
with eyes
that see only the good in people;
with a mind
always open to others' opinions;
with a heart
always caring of their concerns.
Teach me to humble myself
even before the lowliest
of Your children,
whose very brokenness
brings them closer
to You.

(LM 1:14)

FINDING GOOD

O loving God,
help me discover
and uncover
all that is good,
all that is positive
in the world.
Camouflaged though they may be,
let me find
those elusive sparks of
holy light.
Let me perceive all the beauty
and truth
hidden within Your Creation.

(LM 1:33)

FINDING GOOD

When I am confronted
with baseness and evil,
let all the bad
fall away before me.
Let all the good and Godliness
that lies hidden
within everyone I meet
shine forth
and emerge
as a grand reflection
of beauty and light.

(LM 1:33)

LOSING CONTROL

Oh how much good
I've lost
in losing control
of my anger;
such a large portion of life,
so much growth
I've let slip from my hands
by allowing my burning thoughts
to get the better of me.
God,
teach me to let go.

(LM 1:68)

MAINTAINING PERSPECTIVE

O God, please help me comprehend
that life in this world is fleeting—
hardly more than a fantasy.
At this moment I am here,
as are those around me.
Where will I be—
where will they be—
in an hour,
in a day,
in a year or in ten?
Help me hold in my mind
an image
of the World that awaits me—
of the Life Eternal
that will follow my stay
in this place of momentary fascination
and reverie.

(LM 1:65)

IN THANKS

My God,
it has taken me time,
but I'm finally learning
to trust You.
When I called, You answered;
when I cried, You sent relief;
when I was in need,
You came through.
You are there for me
in every instance.
I need only
look, think, and understand,
and I can always find You;
there You are,
always ready to help.
Thank You, God,
for waiting for me.

(LM 1:225)

5

WILL

WILL

WANTING TO WANT

In one of his most powerful statements, Rebbe Nachman unequivocally characterizes that facet of the human psyche which functions below the threshold of consciousness.

A young man was bemoaning the difficulties he was encountering in his attempts to come closer to God. "But I really want to be a good Jew!" he insisted to Rebbe Nachman.

"But," said the Rebbe, "do you really *want* to want?!"

***

IN PRAISE

God, You've given me
the physical, emotional
and spiritual will
to overcome so many obstacles
that have risen before me.
How many times have I faced
what I perceived to be
impossible, hopeless situations
and withstood them—
and discovered creative solutions
through which to surmount
and master them.
You've strengthened me
again and again.
I know that You
will never fail me.

(LM 1:74)

IN GOD'S WILL

Merciful God,
I know how very much
You care for me;
You've made me
"in accordance with Your Will."
Why then don't I always want
to be
that which You've made me?
Why do I so often fall short
of all that
You want me to be?

IN GOD'S WILL

God, I want
to be so many things,
to do so much,
to achieve so endlessly—
but can anyone
be everything,
do everything,
have everything?
You alone understand
the fragile balance of my soul.
You've invested in me
the potential
to make of that balance
a perfect creation.
Now help me fashion myself
into just such a creation,
"in accordance with Your Will."

(LM 1:17)

OVERCOMING NEGATIVE TRAITS

O God,
help me perfect
every element
of my humanness.
Help me overcome
all my negative traits,
all my evil motivations.
Teach me to turn bad
into good.

BUILDING GOOD TRAITS

Help me grow;
teach me to strive for
a soul that is
pure and flawless.
Let my every characteristic be
impervious to evil.
Surely then I can hope
that I—
in my very humanness—
might merge with the holiness
of Your Existence.

(LM 1:8)

PERFECTION OF THE SOUL

God, perfect God—
You created me
destined for perfection;
how far have I wandered
from that destiny!
How much of my purity
have I squandered
through careless, thoughtless,
self-centered behavior—
behavior wanting in morality
and holiness.

THE SOUL'S RECOVERY

There must be a way
I can regain
decency and virtue.
There must be a way
I can recapture
the purity and perfection
of my soul.
God,
lead me there;
don't turn me away.
Open Your Hands
and welcome me back.

(LM 1:19)

THE GIFT OF FREE WILL

God of wonders,
You've given me
the most wonderful
of all gifts—
the gift of free will.
May my will never deviate
from Your holy Will.
Guide me always,
so that all the choices I make
are good ones—
choices that are
in harmony with Your Will,
as long as I live.

(LM 1:190)

A WORLD OF RESPONSIBILITY

Architect of the world,
Author of her story,
grant me the courage
to participate
in the world's design,
to join
in the unfolding of her story.
How I want
to share
in the responsibility
of this world—
to pray for her welfare,
to care for her needs,
to safeguard her treasures,
to work for her rectification.

(LM 1:5)

SELF-RENEWAL

Dear God,
teach me to begin anew—
to renew myself
along with all of Creation,
just as You renew
the entire world
each day.
Show me how I can
break free
of
the constraints of my habits,
the restraints of my insecurities,
the shackles of my unwarranted fears.

A FRESH START

Teach me, dear God,
to make a fresh start;
to break yesterday's patterns;
to stop telling myself
I can't—
when I can,
I'm not—
when I am,
I'm stuck—
when I'm eminently free.

(LM 1:76)

THE WAY HOME

Center of all existence,
help me find the way
to that sacred sanctuary
within myself,
to that precious center of my existence.
Help me discover
my place in the world—
that space where I truly belong,
that space which belongs
unconditionally to me.
Dear God,
I've wandered for so very long.
Help me find my way
home.

(LM 1:188)

HEALING MY LIFE

Dear God,
what a mess I've made of my life—
a hopeless mess.
How will I ever right
all that I've wronged,
restore all that I've ruined,
fix all that I've destroyed?
Only You can help me,
dear God.
If You don't help me,
what hope is there?
Help me
and heal my life.

(LM 1:29)

REACHING FOR WHOLENESS

Compassionate God,
Healer of my body,
Healer of my soul,
heal me.
Strengthen my ailing body;
soothe my aching heart;
mend my shattered existence.
Make me whole.

(LM 1:163)

REJUVENATION

Master of the World,
You know the bitterness
of my anguished heart,
of my painful wounds,
of my afflicted soul.
It is more than I can bear!
I beg You:
Soften and sweeten
the bitterness.
Give me strength
and courage,
for my remedy too
must certainly be bitter;
my rejuvenation
will not come easily.
Healer of all,
heal me.

(LM 1:27)

A MEASURE OF ETERNITY

Eternal God,
grant me a measure of eternity;
lend some permanence
to this temporal life of mine.
Grant health,
happiness
and long life
to my children,
and to their children.
As long as they live,
some part of myself
will survive;
something of me
will live on in this world.
Give me life, dear God,
and life to those who come after me.

(LM 2:68)

CHILDREN

Loving God,
what is more precious
than our children?
Is there any treasure that can be
more beloved,
more pure
than those cherished souls
we have brought into the world?
Help me guide them well,
dear God,
and help them accept my guidance.
Help them lead their lives
with faith,
wisdom
and truth.

(LM 2:7)

LETTING GO

Dear God,
help me grow old
with dignity and wisdom.
As the twilight years
cast their shadow upon me,
help my mind remain clear—
at peace with the world
and with itself.
Let me learn to let go
of my bonds with this world—
of my need for
honor and status;
of my attraction to
physical indulgences;
of my envy of others;
of my regrets
over all that might have been.

AGELESS AGING

Teach me, God,
to live out my days
focused on
all that is meaningful in life.
As unaccountable aches and pains
multiply,
as memory and retention
fade,
teach me to relate to my physical existence
with an ever-expanding recognition
of its transient nature;
teach me to relate to my soul
with an ever-expanding awareness
of her eternal nature
and ageless worth.

(LM 2:10)

APPROACHING GOD

My soul thirsts for You
O God—
will I ever deserve
to feel You beside me?
There are so many obstacles
that keep me
from being what I want to be—
a good person,
a God-conscious person—
but only I myself
can change this.
Help me make the effort
to come closer to You.
Help me long
and yearn
and strive
for Your nearness.

(LM 1:115)

TRUE TO SELF

My God,
teach me to be true
to myself.
Never let me be swayed
by the approval
or the disapproval
of others.
Help me learn to depend
on no one but You,
and to look nowhere
but within
to come to know
my true self—
that person I really am.

(LM 1:66)

IN TUNE WITH GOD

O dear God,
be with me,
and help me
strive to come close—
to be fully committed
to You.
Let every part of me
—physical, emotional and spiritual—
join
in focused determination
to fulfill Your Will.
May my thoughts,
my emotions,
my words,
and all my actions
be wholly in tune
with You.

(LM 1:23)

IN THANKS

O God,
I can never thank You enough
for leading me toward
the path to wholeness
in life:
You've shown me how
to make my desires
akin to Your Will.
The way
to rectification and renewal,
to deep solace and healing,
to meaning and eternal tranquility—
is only through
actively seeking
Your Will.
Thank You, God, for leading me
to that understanding.

(LM 1:268)

WHO WAS REBBE NACHMANOF BRESLOV?

Rebbe Nachman of Breslov was born in 1772, in the Ukrainian village of Medzeboz. A great-grandson of Rabbi Israel Baal Shem Tov, founder of the Hasidic movement, Rebbe Nachman attained outstanding levels of saintliness and wisdom. At home in the furthest reaches of Kabbalah mysticism, while at the same time artlessly practical and to-the-point, he taught honesty, simplicity, and faith. He wove wondrous tales of princesses, giants, beggars, and emperors.... He spoke of healing and wholeness ... of being alive!

Rebbe Nachman attracted a devoted following, simple folk and scholars alike, who looked to him as "the Rebbe," their prime source of spiritual guidance and support. Even after his passing in 1810, Rebbe Nachman's influence remained potent. His teachings spread by word of mouth and through his writings. His followers continued to look to his lessons for guidance and inspiration. Today, the movement he initiated is vibrant and growing. Far beyond these circles, Rebbe Nachman's supreme optimism and down-to-earth wisdom have made him one of the most often-quoted and studied Jewish teachers of all time.

Rebbe Nachman lived at what must be considered one of human history's most significant turning points. His lifetime spanned the beginnings of the Industrial Revolution, the American War of Independence, and the French Revolution. Goethe, Kant, Byron, Beethoven, and Mozart were all active during the Rebbe's generation. In an era poised for a paradigm shift that would engender great reason but also profound doubt, an unparalleled conquering of external frontiers but also an unprecedented inner void, Rebbe Nachman put his finger on the pulse of the dawning age and said: "I'll tell you a secret: Great atheism is coming into the world...."

Today, almost two hundred years later, estrangement from God is paralleled in another form of "great atheism"—in an alienation from self.

Addressing an age in which feelings of emptiness would predominate, Rebbe Nachman developed a universal doctrine that speaks to the spiritually-seeking, as well as to anyone facing the problems of everyday living. His message, one of hope and joy, teaches that even where the black-hole-of-self seems most impenetrable, sparks of light are waiting to be released. His words of inspiration reach out to the faithful of any faith, to the not-so-faithful, and even to those with no faith at all.

ABOUT THE BRESLOV RESEARCH INSTITUTE

Rebbe Nachman was only 38 years old when he passed away in 1810. Yet shortly before his passing, he told his followers that his influence would endure long afterwards. "My light will burn until the days of the Mashiach [Messiah]." Generations of readers have been enthralled and inspired by his writings, which have been explored and interpreted by leading scholars around the globe.

The growing interest in Rebbe Nachman from all sectors—academia and laymen alike—led to the establishment of the Breslov Research Institute in Jerusalem in 1979. Since then a team of scholars has been engaged in research into the texts, oral traditions, and music of the Breslov movement. The purpose of the Institute is to publish authoritative translations, commentaries, and general works on Breslov Hasidut. Projects also include the recording of Breslov songs and melodies on cassettes and in music book form.

Offices and representatives of the Breslov Research Institute:

Israel:

Breslov Research Institute
P.O. Box 5370

Jerusalem, Israel
Tel: (011-9722) 582-4641
Fax: (011-9722) 582-5542
www.breslov.org

North America:

Breslov Research Institute
P.O. Box 587
Monsey, NY 10952-0587
Tel: (845) 425-4258
Fax (845) 425-30181
www.breslov.org

Breslov books may be ordered directly from these offices or from Jewish Lights Publishing. Ordering information is provided at the end of this book.

BOOKS FROM THE BRESLOV RESEARCH INSTITUTE...

RABBI NACHMAN'S STORIES
Translated by *Rabbi Aryeh Kaplan*
6x9, 552 pages, HC. Bibliography, Index.

ANATOMY OF THE SOUL
by *Chaim Kramer*
Edited by *Avraham Sutton*
6x9, 364 pages, HC. Appendices.

CROSSING THE NARROW BRIDGE A Practical Guide to Rebbe Nachman's Teachings
by *Chaim Kramer*
Edited by *Moshe Mykoff*
5 1/2x8 1/2, 452 pages, HC. Appendices.

RABBI NACHMAN'S WISDOM
Translated by *Rabbi Aryeh Kaplan*
Edited by *Rabbi Zvi Aryeh Rosenfeld*
6x9, 486 pages, HC. Appendices, Index.

THE BRESLOV HAGGADAH
Compiled and translated by *Rabbi Yehoshua Starret* and *Chaim Kramer*
Edited by *Moshe Mykoffe*
6 1/2x9 1/2, 256 pages, HC. Appendices3

ABOUT JEWISH LIGHTS PUBLISHING

People of all faiths and backgrounds yearn for books that attract, engage, educate, and spiritually inspire.

Our principal goal is to stimulate thought and help all people learn about who the Jewish People are, where they come from, and what the future can be made to hold. While people of our diverse Jewish heritage are the primary audience, our books speak to people in the Christian world as well and will broaden their understanding of Judaism and the roots of their own faith.

We bring to you authors who are at the forefront of spiritual thought and experience. While each has something different to say, they all say it in a voice that you can hear. Our books are designed to welcome you and then to engage, stimulate, and inspire. We judge our success not only by whether or not our books are beautiful and commercially successful, but by whether or not they make a difference in your life.

**AVAILABLE FROM BETTER BOOKSTORES.
TRY YOUR BOOKSTORE FIRST.**

Spirituality/Inspiration/Kabbalah

ZOHAR
Annotated & Explained
Translation and annotation by *Daniel C. Matt*

(A SkyLight Paths Book)

**THE JEWISH LIGHTS
SPIRITUALITY HANDBOOK
A Guide to Understanding, Exploring
& Living a Spiritual Life**
Edited by *Stuart M. Matlins*

MAKING PRAYER REAL
**Leading Jewish Spiritual Voices on Why Prayer
Is Difficult and What to Do about It**
by *Rabbi Mike Comins*

**EHYEH
A Kabbalah for Tomorrow**
by *Arthur Green*

Phone, fax, e-mail or mail orders to:
JEWISH LIGHTS Publishing
Sunset Farm Offices, Route 4, P.O. Box 237
Woodstock, Vermont 05091
Tel: (802) 457-4000 • Fax: (802) 457-4004 (24-hour)
sales@jewishlights.com
Credit card orders: (800) 962-4544 (8:30AM–5:30PM EST M–F)
Generous discounts on quantity orders. SATISFACTION GUARANTEED. Prices subject to change.
www.jewishlights.com

Spirituality/Inspiration/Kabbalah

SEEK MY FACE
A Jewish Mystical Theology
by *Arthur Green*

A FORMULA FOR PROPER LIVING
Practical Lessons from Life and Torah
by *Abraham J. Twerski, MD*

TANYA, THE MASTERPIECE
OF HASIDIC WISDOM
Selections Annotated & Explained
Translation and annotation by *Rabbi Rami Shapiro*
Foreword by *Rabbi Zalman M. Schachter-Shalomi*

HAPPINESS AND THE HUMAN SPIRIT
The Spirituality of Becoming
the Best You Can Be
by *Abraham J. Twerski, MD*

TWELVE JEWISH STEPS TO RECOVERY, 2ND ED.
A Personal Guide to Turning from
Alcoholism and Other Addictions—Drugs,
Food, Gambling, Sex...
by *Rabbi Kerry M. Olitzky* and *Stuart A. Copans, MD*
Preface by *Abraham J. Twerski, MD*
Introduction by *Rabbi Sheldon Zimmerman*
Illustrated by *Maty Grünberg*

Spiritual Inspiration

THESE ARE THE WORDS, 2ND ED.
A Vocabulary of Jewish Spiritual Life
by *Arthur Green*

THE SABBATH SOUL
Mystical Reflections on the Transformative
Power of Holy Time
Selection, translation and commentary by
Eitan Fishbane, PhD

GOD'S TO-DO LIST
103 Ways to Be an Angel
and Do God's Work on Earth
by *Dr. Ron Wolfson*

SACRED INTENTIONS
Morning Inspiration to Strengthen the Spirit,
Based on Jewish Wisdom
by *Rabbi Kerry M. Olitzky* and
Rabbi Lori Forman-Jacobi

FILLING WORDS WITH LIGHT
Hasidic and Mystical Reflections
on Jewish Prayer
by *Lawrence Kushner* and *Nehemia Polen*

Spiritual Inspiration for Children

MULTICULTURAL, NONSECTARIAN, NONDENOMINATIONAL
Endorsed by Protestant, Catholic and Jewish religious leaders

Books by Sandy Eisenberg Sasso

GOD'S PAINTBRUSH　　　　　*For ages 4 & up*
Invites children to encounter God openly in their lives.

For ages 4 & up　　　　　**IN GOD'S NAME**
A vibrant fable about the search for God's name.

BUT GOD REMEMBERED　　　*For ages 8 & up*
Stories of Women from Creation
to the Promised Land

For ages 5 & up　　　　　**CAIN & ABEL**
Finding the Fruits of Peace

AROUND THE WORLD　　　　*For ages 3–6*
IN ONE SHABBAT
Jewish People Celebrate the Sabbath Together
by *Durga Yael Bernhard*

For ages 4 & up　　**BECAUSE NOTHING LOOKS**
LIKE GOD
by *Lawrence and Karen Kushner*

Add Greater Meaning to Your Life

THE WOMEN'S TORAH COMMENTARY
New Insights from Women Rabbis
on the 54 Weekly Torah Portions
Edited by *Rabbi Elyse Goldstein*

THE MODERN MEN'S TORAH COMMENTARY
New Insights from Jewish Men on
the 54 Weekly Torah Portions
Edited by *Rabbi Jeffrey K. Salkin*

THE WAY INTO THE
VARIETIES OF JEWISHNESS
by *Sylvia Barack Fishman, PhD*

A DREAM OF ZION
American Jews Reflect on
Why Israel Matters to Them
Edited by *Rabbi Jeffrey K. Salkin*

THE TORAH REVOLUTION
Fourteen Truths That Changed the World
by *Rabbi Reuven Hammer, PhD*

Books by Lawrence Kushner

I'M GOD; YOU'RE NOT
Observations on Organized Religion
& Other Disguises of the Ego

INVISIBLE LINES OF CONNECTION
Sacred Stories of the Ordinary

HONEY FROM THE ROCK
An Introduction to Jewish Mysticism

THE BOOK OF WORDS
Talking Spiritual Life, Living Spiritual Talk

THE BOOK OF LETTERS
A Mystical Hebrew Alphabet
In calligraphy by the author

GOD WAS IN THIS PLACE & I, i
DID NOT KNOW
Finding Self, Spirituality & Ultimate Meaning

EYES REMADE FOR WONDER
The Way of Jewish Mysticism and Sacred Living
A Lawrence Kushner Reader

Add Greater Meaning to Your Life

THE SACRED ART OF LOVINGKINDNESS
Preparing to Practice
by *Rabbi Rami Shapiro*; Foreword by *Marcia Ford*

DISCOVERING JEWISH MEDITATION,
2ND ED.
Instruction & Guidance for Learning an
Ancient Spiritual Practice
by *Nan Fink Gefen, PhD*

I AM JEWISH
Personal Reflections Inspired by the Last
Words of Daniel Pearl
Edited by *Judea* and *Ruth Pearl*

THE WAY INTO *TIKKUN OLAM*
(REPAIRING THE WORLD)
by *Rabbi Elliot N. Dorff, PhD*

ISRAEL—A SPIRITUAL TRAVEL GUIDE,
2ND ED.
A Companion for the Modern Jewish Pilgrim
by *Rabbi Lawrence A. Hoffman*

120

More Wisdom from the Hasidic Masters

GOD IN ALL MOMENTS
Mystical & Practical Spiritual Wisdom from
Hasidic Masters
Edited and translated by *Or N. Rose*
with *Ebn D. Leader*

TORMENTED MASTER
The Life and Spiritual Quest
of Rabbi Nahman of Bratslav
by *Arthur Green*

YOUR WORD IS FIRE
The Hasidic Masters on Contemplative Prayer
Edited and translated with a new introduction by
Arthur Green and *Barry W. Holtz*

THE WAY INTO
JEWISH MYSTICAL TRADITION
by *Lawrence Kushner*

Phone, fax, e-mail or mail orders to:
JEWISH LIGHTS Publishing
Sunset Farm Offices, Route 4, P.O. Box 237
Woodstock, Vermont 05091
Tel: (802) 457-4000 • Fax: (802) 457-4004 (24-hour)
sales@jewishlights.com
Credit card orders: **(800) 962-4544** (8:30AM–5:30PM EST M–F)
Generous discounts on quantity orders. SATISFACTION GUARANTEED. Prices subject to change.
www.jewishlights.com

FRONT COVER FLAP

**"When you pray, hold nothing
back from God. Pour out your
heart with honest openness, as if
you were speaking to your very
best friend."**

—Rebbe Nachman of Breslov (1772–1810)

A "little treasure" of prayers that will open your heart
and soul and give voice to your deepest yearnings.
Using the startling wisdom of Rebbe Nachman of
Breslov, written two hundred years ago, *The Gentle
Weapon* will help you talk with God and enable you
to hear your own voice as well.

This spiritual gem makes a loving gift to friends,
family, or to ourselves when words of comfort are
what's needed the most.

**"An ideal and loving gift to anyone who needs
to pray, needs to learn to pray, or needs comfort
to get through the days' trials and tribulations."**

—*Options*

BACK COVER FLAP

Also available

The Empty Chair: Finding Hope and Joy

Timeless Wisdom from a Hasidic Master, Rebbe Nachman of Breslov

A treasury of aphorisms and advice for living joyously and spiritually today, to help us move from stress and sadness to hope and joy.

4x6, 128 pp, Deluxe Paperback

Praise for
The Empty Chair: Finding Hope and Joy

***

"For anyone of any faith, this is a book of healing and wholeness, of being alive!"

—*Bookviews*

"A wondrous collection of aphorisms."

—*Publishers Weekly*

BACK COVER MATERIAL

The Gentle Weapon

*Prayers for Everyday
and Not-So-Everyday Moments*

***

"Life makes warriors of us all.
To emerge the victors, we must arm
ourselves with the most potent of weapons.
That weapon is prayer."
—*Rebbe Nachman of Breslov*

***

The "gentle weapon" of prayer can ease the soul and strengthen the heart, while bringing us closer to God and to a deeper understanding of ourselves.

Two hundred years after he lived, the warm insights and generous wisdom of Rebbe Nachman of Breslov (1772–1810) continue to be a source of comfort for those in search of an uplifting perspective on life.

126

Made in the USA
Las Vegas, NV
25 October 2021